# I AM NOT YOUR FINAL GIRL

# I AM NOT YOUR FINAL GIRL

poems

Claire C. Holland

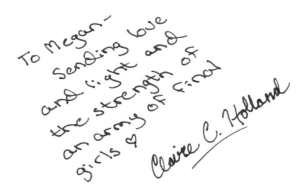

To Megan—
Sending love
and light and
the strength of
an army of Final
girls ♥

Claire C. Holland

GLASSPOET PRESS | LOS ANGELES

Published by GlassPoet Press, Los Angeles, CA 91607

www.clairecholland.com

Book Layout © 2017 BookDesignTemplates.com

Cover design by Claire C. Holland

Cover fonts © Thomas W. Otto, Norfok.com

Cover edited with brushes from Brusheezy.com

I Am Not Your Final Girl/ Claire C. Holland. -- 1st ed.

ISBN-13: 978-0692966631

ISBN-10: 0692966633

*To my mom,*

*for making me a reader,*

*and to my dad,*

*for making me a writer.*

# Contents

# Destruction

# Transformation

# Introduction

Too much bad has happened in the last year, and I'm tired.

Tired of watching a racist, misogynist old white man abuse the most powerful office in America. Tired of old white men in general – especially the ones trying to tell me what to do with my body, as if they have a clue. Tired of listening to rich men negotiate and renegotiate my humanity. The way they act like it's up for debate.

Tired of smiling sweetly, or not smiling enough, or smiling *too* sweetly. Tired of all the little indignities, of gritting my teeth and silently walking on every time a man considers it his right to comment on my face, my body, my choice of clothes. Tired of holding keys in my fists like sad little brass knuckles.

Tired of hearing the same stories, over and over again, of women being harmed and treated like playthings by men with just enough power to take advantage. Tired of feeling a sense of recognition, low and stony in the pit of the stomach, every time I hear one of these stories. Like I've been there, in some other life or just months ago.

Tired of hearing that other people are tired of these stories, when I know just how essential they are. Knowing that they must be spoken aloud, over and over again, like a melody or mantra that maybe – if we say it enough, if we refuse to shut up – will become a part of our collective consciousness. A part we can no longer ignore, or call urban myth.

I'm tired, but I draw strength from the many strong women around me, both real and fictional. Women like Maxine Waters, Danica Roem, Elizabeth Warren. Or Tarana Burke, Anita Hill, and

Dylan Farrow. From the organizers of the Women's March and the #MeToo movement to the women running for office for the first time – I could go on, and the list would never be complete, because the number of women working to change the norm in America and the world is evergrowing. I am indebted to so many women simply for giving me hope since the 2016 election.

There are other women, too, who have inspired and galvanized me throughout my life. I grew up loving horror movies, and I've always felt drawn to the "final girls" in these movies – the girls who fought tooth and nail to survive until the end. I've often looked to these women for courage, but never more so than now. I wrote a whole book trying to channel that fight into something I could use myself.

These are not all final girls, in the strictest sense. The term "horror heroine" is coming into vogue, and it seems more appropriate since things don't always end well for strong, angry women. Not all the women in this book are the survivors, much as I wish they were. They're final girls in my heart, though, and I hold them closest. These are the women I feel raging inside me, the women whose pain and fury help me deal with my own darkest moments. They show me I can be stronger. They show me that I'm not alone. I cherish them all for going down fighting, and for taking a piece of their oppressors as they go.

If the year since that fateful election has taught me anything, it's that real women are final girls, and so much more. We are more than a trope. We're strong and slutty, quiet and confident, outspoken and sarcastic and we don't feel like smiling because we have work to do. We defy definition. And we're not going down without a fight.

# Assault

# Rosemary
### *Rosemary's Baby* (1968)

It always begins with the good intentions
of men.

Her body on the deck of a ship,
inert and shining.

The way he carried her down the hall,
like a child,
like a duffel bag.
The promises he made when he put her
to bed.

> *This is for us,*
he probably said.

Then in the morning,
how he could look at her only
sideways. How he grinned

sheepishly at her half-asked question
> *—you... while I was out?—*
then shrugged, brushed his teeth,
got dressed.

Meanwhile, she still dreams
of the ship,

of cold waves lapping at unsheltered thighs.
Still wonders at the scratches
marking her skin.

She's not so naive. She senses,
in the organ-deep way women sense things:
it's not the Devil
you need to worry about,

but the devil you know.

## The Female (Part I)
*Under the Skin* (2013)

The thing that rips
you open

like a burlap sack,
spilling

black stars, an infinity
of humanity,

your empathy.

It's that sad,
fragile,

beautiful thing
that will ruin you.

## Jennifer
### *I Spit on Your Grave* (1978)

There are moments, black ice

moments, that glitter and burn

and turn in the mind like

crystal, too bright and sharp

to touch. The half-split second,

a cracked open chasm between

then and now, *this* and *that*, his hand

around her ankle. What happens

next. She has teeth and claws

and fight in this fight, but it will

mean nothing to a man who says

    *I like a girl with spirit*

when what he means is

    *I like a girl that can break.*

# Carol
## *Repulsion* (1965)

If we were able to evolve as we
wished, women would all
have wings.

We would not be tethered
to anything: the earth,
that somber apartment,

and all the things we cannot
escape from inside
our ponderous bodies.

I would give her this, if
I could. The witch-like ability
to burst

into a cloud of feathers,
to soar to the ceiling and out
the window, away.

Some women never adapt
to walls that close
in like grabbing hands,

and to hands that grab.

## Sara
### *The Descent* (2005)

The darkness isn't so bad.
Like a cool velvet
blanket
draped over her shoulders,
her head,
her
face.

It presses her eyelids
closed,
like fingers.
When she opens
them, the room is bathed
in gentle
golden light,
church light, birthday
cake light.
And she thinks,

*This is all I ever wanted.*
To be trapped in this place
with you.

But

in the darkness
the night monsters
come. And
it is always dark down here.
She knows this.

The crystal light is gone
with a blink, and
she is alone.
Mostly.
She can hear them coming
from very far away,

the clickings
of their forked
and slimy tongues. Greasy bodies
wriggling
down dank tunnels,
and scrabbling over stones.
She lies
stock-still, her cheek

in the wet dirt.
The ghosts are worse.
They never go away, only wait
for perfect
moments
to throttle her windpipe, choke
off her

breath,
make her sputter
and cough, like they want
her to get caught. See her torn
into rags
of skin
and sinew.
Of course, they do.

She wonders
what's worse:

To be slit down your belly
like a fish,
or to recognize this cage.
So black and
damp, and filled
with shiny
bones.

## Jesse
*The Neon Demon* (2016)

Naked she glitters, a body cut

from marble, stony and white,

a sun turned inside out

and set to glowing, exploding.

Her prettiness is a mantra she tells

herself in the motel mirror,

a crown of silver and wildflowers,

she wears it as armor against

his wolf smile. There's a trap,

an accusation there, a snare ready

and taut for loose limbs.

## Martha
### *Martha Marcy May Marlene* (2011)

It's a trick of the light,
the way it bleeds
from one day, place, thought
into another.
How it cuts through
glass like a knife, uncloaks
darkness
only to reveal shadow.

You can't blame her for being confused.

There's a hand, dust-dry
and bony,
sliding up
underneath her dress. And it happens
so slowly, so artfully,
she forgets she never said yes.
Forgets this body

and brain are hers to keep.
Even now that she's gone, a streak
of white cutting
through the woods
like a deer,
she feels his breath on her neck.
Touches the unseen imprint
of his fingers

white-hot on her wrist.
The farther away she gets.
Forgets her own name, but not
how it felt
—how it feels—
to be nothing but his
idea of her.
A picture on his shelf.

# Carla
## *The Entity* (1982)

I got tired of hearing it was my fault.
I think we all do. That's the crux of it,
the cross that certain people bear—
       *women*, doctors sneer like it's a dirty word and
       then they take your pain and put it in a bottle
       with a number on it.

And the number's always low, did you notice
that? Maybe because pain is relative, but
when pain *is* your relative, your nasty bedfellow,
it's hard to see them label it three when
your mind is screaming twelve,
when it's ticking off time—

hands on your ankles like shackles, like
something that brings to mind the speculum
for no reason you can grasp in this moment,
your breast being kneaded like so much dough,
it's utilitarian, it's a means to an end, an end
that doesn't come but stretches, stretches on—

like pieces of yourself that are gone now forever.
I got tired of hearing it was my fault, that's all.
This constant suffering, like I was Eve
holding out the apple to spite myself. Aren't I
my own woman? Or is that not enough?
They look at me like I'm hiding something.

# Sally
*The Texas Chain Saw Massacre* **(1974)**

Her face,
bathed in blood. Her smile,
crazed.
The sounds she makes
as she escapes.

There is nothing else in this world
like realizing
you're going to live
and not being sure
you can.

# Laurie
## *Halloween* (1978)

I ask you to tell me of a town
where this hasn't happened,
where some brute dressed in black

hasn't donned a mask, shadowed
a woman, called himself a monster
to blot out his own mortality.

Tell me why I should mythologize
this. Let his shape grow larger
than the women crouched

with coat hangers, with makeshift
daggers as sturdy as their hearts?
Something can be vulnerable

and powerful both at once, but
you cannot understand this,
and I have grown so weary trying

to explain. You say you want
to protect us, but the method, blunt
pills forced to mouths, a technique

for hysteria, is all wrong. It abrades.
White fences are only made of wood,
they splinter so easily.

# Possession

# Anna
## *Possession* (1981)

A woman's body was made for this,
for birthing, for enduring

hours of pulsating pain, but no birth,
no ingress into this world should hurt

this much. A blade in her back,
it threatens to bubble up from inside,

to pour from her prone and twisting
body, everywhere, frothing

into cracks in the cement, heavy
like paint. And so she thrashes, smashes

her head against the tunnel walls
like a dervish, a devil woman demented

and godlike, with her too-many arms
waving, a container for grief and this other

thing she cannot name. A broken
discontent, willing itself to life.

# Rachel
## *The Ring* (2002)

It starts
at the back of her throat.
An itch
or tickle,
like torn nails
stroking
the tender, wet membrane
behind her tongue.

Like ragged edges
of a rope,
scraping

from inside.
As the days pass-
*one two three*
*four five six*
-marked by fiery sunsets
and green-stained
nights,

she feels it.
Not just in her, but
around her,
a haze of disease
like flies.
Her skin turns pale
and dimpled.
Wetter.

Her brain, too,
feels soggy,
sodden.

Then there are the horses.
She sees them
in her dreams, eyes
ringed white.
She sees
they are afraid
of her.

What is it
about their faces?
Those long Roman
noses
and lateral eyes.

The way they watch.
How they see.

They know she has
something,
something queasy
and bilious.
They know she's looking
to pass it on.

And she will.
And it's not so easy
as coughing on a stranger,
or even sharing
a needle.
It's filthy,

corporeal work.
But it's instinct, fleshly
instinct,
that drives her
like a rat from water.
To save
herself.

Still, at night
she sees the horses.
Feels their cold gaze
on her skin.

What is it
about their faces?

# Bea
### *Honeymoon* (2014)

She wonders if the question
is inevitable.

> *What happened?*

If every woman
goes through this.

> *My wife doesn't act this way.*

How he needles her,
questions each part of her, the way she
talks and dresses.

> *You smell the same. You taste
> the same.*

And when he ties her to the bed,
gropes her,
interrogates her
with that baffled look on his face—

> *But you're different.
> You're different.*

—she almost laughs at him
out loud.
Because she has changed.

Did he really think she wouldn't?

## Shideh
### *Under the Shadow* (2016)

Separate yourself, like sliding wire through
clay. Divide your organs - heart, lungs, tongue,
and brain. You think you need them all?
You'd be shocked what a woman can live
without. We're like roaches, we thrive,

pull our tired bodies through war, things
we never asked for, with children strapped
to our backs. Now don't forget the smaller bits:
tonsils, gallbladder. Your ovaries, your veins.
A box for bile, another to keep you sane. Make

a plan. Mark each box with an *x* and let it sit.
Let it fester in the dark, grow mold, grow rabid
with disuse. Your personality is apartments,
doors that can be closed. When they come
they'll take pieces, they can't carry it all.

They can't change you, too much. Can't know
what you do at home. Just try not to howl,
or shudder, when you see: when it happens to us
it's for the best, but when it happens to them
it's tragedy.

# Heather
*The Woods* (2006)

Drink down dominion like milk,
let it slither along the throat, that hard

muscle for gulping. It's been saved
for nothing but

to whisper in hallways, to cover the mouth
with deft fingers, the note cut off.

Sample each drop, bring it
to your neck, perfume. It brings the scent

of nettle and something like a secret,
but more formidable. It invites.

If you follow into the thicket, don't
forget to take up the ax.

# Ginger
*Ginger Snaps* (2000)

It was October, of course,
and balmier than seemed right. When the moon
makes bodies dark.

First were the dogs,
their bodies splintered, oozing, littered
across green lawns.
Then things got worse.

I got cursed, in every way a woman can.

You kill yourself, over and over, to be different.
Poisoned tea parties, impalements. Domestic chores
are the death of you. Then this.

    *Run ladies. Bounce!*

You can't trust your body.

    *I bet she's good to go.*

Unless you embrace it.

Your wicked spine, the knobby newness
of certain parts. The drive for something that feels
like desire. Like sex, delicious.

But it's so much more. More
than you ever would have thought
to ask for, because you're a girl and girls don't
play at death. We don't fantasize.

Until we do.

You might say things didn't end well,
but I had fun. Ask anyone.

## Thomasin
### *The Witch* (2015)

She is so tired of waiting
—aren't you?—
for the world to become good
and tolerable and kind.

To be seen,
not for the swell of her breasts,
or the curve of childbearing
hips,

not for the sin of her unbridled
hair, or the youthful flush
on her cheek.
To be seen,

without suspicion.
She is so tired
of waiting.
She won't do it anymore.

# Molly
*Lovely Molly* (2011)

They said the Devil is a cloven-
hoofed thing,

a lumbering thing, all misshapen
edges and inelegant lines. But

when he materializes
from some fog — the woods or

her bramble-full, muddied brain —
he is reptilian, smooth and glistening,

dark crystal scaled. He is
enchanting. He is threaded

like tugging at her seams, so ready
to split, to make her a thing cleaved

in half. A moral: the way he wraps
her in chilly moss, so cold

from predawn light it feels like fire
against her skin. How the marking

of her skin means faith, means
acceptance, means nothing

can mark her inflamed skin again
after his touch.

## Sarah
*The Craft* (1996)

It doesn't always end this way, a girl strapped
to the bed, her wrists purpled, eyes trained

on something gone. Believe me. Every day before
this one was filled with flocks of butterflies,

clutched hands, nights brimming with secrets we told
each other like spells. The air crackled

with our potential, neon and electric. And if
we failed at tying our hands together in prayer,

that's not permission to turn away. Watch for me,
even when it's moonless. I'll throw a spark.

# Nola
### *The Brood* (1979)

Dress me in pale blue and wrap
my hands in gauze.

Encircle my belly with chains

of flowers.

I know your thoughts.

This bloody
exploit, this motherhood,

is too dirty for you to brave.
Stash it behind shutters,

behind padded walls
of cotton stuffing our ears

and mouths.

The law believes in motherhood,
in theory.

Put to practice,
and you are all recoil,

all kickback.

Don't you want to come with me?

I thought you liked
loaded weapons.

# Destruction

## Francisca
*The Eyes of My Mother* (2016)

Wait: breach my body like I did

yours, like the whale puncturing the ocean or

metal defying the rind; your skin. I hold it

beneath my fingernails. I hold it in a bathtub,

but it does not quicken. How did I grow

so motherless? Blood is black and barely

shows, wait. I am uninhabited.

## Iris and Rose
*We Are What We Are* (2013)

Queasy sound of ripping,
of flesh and gristle grinding,
churning,
aching

between pearl teeth.
Who would imagine any girl's
teeth could do so much
damage:

drag skin from muscle,
and muscle from bone like
pulling apart sheaves
of paper.

They're not cannibals, though.
More like sin-eaters, and watch
how they devour.

Think, how long we've been forced
to consume
these sins of our fathers.

## India
*Stoker* (2013)

She touches tender parts of herself
in the shower,
remembers the sound,
the snapping of his neck.
How it felt like power.

## Mary
*American Mary* **(2012)**

Teeth split
    and salvaged,

spilt on the tongue of words
spoken

    and spoken almost
louder

than the wailing,
her eyes. Hew

his tongue   with thread.

Remove the limbs.

With numbness,
    a backbone

to hold her

up.

There's more than one
              way

to make a man   to make
a woman.

## Amelia
### *The Babadook* (2014)

Lady Macbeth could have dashed a child's sleeping
head against a cinder block wall, if she had

one. Not only watched the skull bloom red,
a slow-burning poppy field set alight,

but found satisfaction in the eruption. The
sudden burst, the quick unfurling

of expectation. And would that have been so bad?
If I could float up above my own tired

bones, change my mother's-hands into talons,
rip out the root of this unrest, would I?

# May
*May* (2002)

A woman who would excavate her own eyes
from their sockets, skewer them like lychee fruit,
balance them on a doll's head just to be seen. A
woman who covets, who collects smooth hands
and swan necks like buttons or scraps of soft old
fabric, lovingly pressed and fondled, sewn into
patterns and strewn on her bedroom floor for the
feast, the dazzling moment when she will swallow
them up like solid honey sliding down her pale,
moving throat. Her hunger is so great, so open,
she has lived through a lifetime of famine and yet
no one will look in her hungry eyes. Instead they
avert their gazes, frown pityingly at one another,
grumble. But she has scissors inside her sleeve
and she clutches them. Look at her. Look at her.

# She
## *Antichrist* (2009)

There is an overwhelming sense of white—
birch trees in the copse, a haze of mist
falling over our faces like a veil. Clouding

my eyes. Concealing you from me.
This is how I've learned to find you
in the fog: follow your condescension, which

tugs at my ribs and yanks at the place
where I keep my grief, hidden and warm
above my belly. Like a leash, bringing me back

to you by inches. This time I will cut it out,
excise that fragile and anemic part of me,
let it ooze heavy as iron from me,

smother it in dirt. I have not learned how
to be obedient, only to hurt myself
as much as you.

## The Female (Part II)
### *Under the Skin* (2013)

Spun out
of light and the bright
mimicry
of sound,
like Venus, she is
perfect, she contains
planets,
universes
of desire inside her
body, yes
she is callous, but
I would not change
her, not now,
and I will
let her run
riotous,
ruinous and wild,
I will let her seduce
you, drown
you in her
mercurial mind until
you choke, yes,
I will
let her have you,
and a thousand others
like you,
if only
to change the
ending
of her story.

# Elsa
*Splice* (2009)

Are men so obsessed with mothering
because they're incapable of it? Or
do they spend their lives making monsters

of themselves
to do the things they can't stomach?
For once I'll remake the world in my image:

I am God and Punisher, Mary full of rage.
My psalms are brain and body, idols
no one can burn or confiscate.

I raise my palms and feel storms conjuring.
Look out the window and my eyes
grow heavy, my gut slaked.

I feel you bob and duck in worship.

# Amy
*Felt* (2014)

Give me muscles, or else I'll make them
myself out of this anger rising
from my throat and bubbling to my skin
like disease I cannot contain any longer.
This is how you make me feel, like some
thing blighted, broken and abnormal.
I rear back my head, thrust my pink
tongue to the sky, make it ugly for you.
I want to hurt you. I want to offend.

I know you'll laugh, and it will feel like
a slap to my jaw. You think I can't, think
my strength seems soft as cotton, spongy
as exposed innards. You think I'm sweet,
candied to cloying, a thing to grab and put
in your mouth until I'm chewed to a pulp
and used up. You're wrong.

I will adorn this body with scars, twist it
until it is sharp, maul it into weaponry.
I will become the fist and gun and bomb
that you have used against me since
the day I was born in this woman's body.
If you find the tenor or shape of my words
unappealing, know that you have made me.
Thank you. I will use all this against you,
and you will not see it coming.

# Transformation

# Jess
### *Black Christmas* (1974)

I am the woman who goes back into the house
because I can't stand waiting on the lawn.

Pick up this steel rod, clench it in both fists,
ignore your pleas to stay. I can't be preserved

in this expectant state, a butterfly in a jar
to make you smile when you look. A creature

made docile with friction.
I can't exist in a way that comforts you.

# Amber
### *Green Room* (2016)

A snake of ice cold
air that breathes its way up
a pant leg like
      gasping.

      I want to speak
the exact outlines
of her, the unknown
contours

of her face in the dark,
her body like water,
her hand on the
      knife.

      Follow, down
the trap door and out
through the spaces
between rafters,

between planks
of wood cobbled
together by broken knuckles
      and red-laced

      rage. It is shocking,
how easy it is to become
the force that infiltrates,
that brings

the sad building
plunging
into ash. To join a lick of flame
          with air.

# Selena
### *28 Days Later* (2002)

A man in a military uniform says
he needs you. Together, you will remake
the fragmented world, carry pieces of it
like lumber on your meaty backs, pile it up
so it towers over this mournful place and blots
out everything we can't bring ourselves
to look at. It feels so good, not to see.

What you won't understand is when he comes
to me and says the same thing. What he's asking for.
Because it's so much more. Because
     *—women mean a future—*
that I don't want a part in. A future built on my body,
pinned beneath yours. Where my pain is overthrown

for your longing, your appetite. You don't know it
yet, but your world is shattered, the remnants
made useless for anything but goring palms
and forging false prophets. I do not mourn it.
Where you saw only cracks, I felt the break,
but you live in it now. You're in here
with me.

# Clarice
*The Silence of the Lambs* (1991)

I have known monsters and I have known men.
I have stood in their long shadows, propped
them up with my own two hands, reached
for their inscrutable faces in the dark. They
are harder to set apart than you know.
Than you will ever know.

But why not try. Slip into my skin, hug it close
to your bones. It is thinner than yours, softer,
easier to mark. You'll want to carry a weapon,
because no matter how hard you work, your
body can't provide cover, and your words
are only words. You'll see what I mean.

Do you feel eyes moving over your body yet?
You will. Cover it with cloth thick as cardboard,
they'll pare it down, peel it away, husk you
like an ear of corn. It happens in seconds,
a cold kick to the gut. You won't be right
every time, but.

# Carrie
*Carrie* (1976)

In a world where fathers reign
like dark clouds casting
shadows from the skyline,
are all of us daughters doomed

to become our mothers?
To string ourselves up, martyrs
on the doorframe, pricked
with knives and other utensils

used yesterday for making dinner?
Or maybe that's how we kill it,
the impulse to serve and say *sorry*
all the time.

It's exhausting, all this
Mary stuff, all this blood and sin
piled on us without our permission.
Intuition is treated like a curse,

because it's not dense and sturdy
as a man's thick fist. They
don't like something that slips
through fingers like water,

but what good are we cast
in white? I'd rather arm myself
in blood than be a pretty statue
to stare at.

# Leah
*Lyle* **(2014)**

Her stomach, swaying in pulse
with breath, with the waves

made by body, by distended belly in
brine. The pool

where it happens, where bodies
are rocked into
     and out of.

Hands can make cradles around
bodies or throats.

## Jay
*It Follows* (2015)

There's a streak of cardinal,
wet and alarming, slapped
on the sunset.

My pastel world's
been written on, scraped into
as gnarled thumbs

in dust. Gnawing dread,
constant worry knuckling hard
at the back of my neck,

I give you up.

Much as I feel you,
your black-eyed stare and coffin
breath, I leave you here,

abandoned and wanting.
See this, how it feels to be left
behind in a pile

of your own slick-sabled outrage.
Let it spurt and surge, seethe
from your neck.

Let you evaporate into earth.

# Mia
*Evil Dead* (2013)

Drowning in red, she is stained. Blue-black
bruised and torn, there are pieces of her
everywhere. A hand in the mud.

A hunk of heart moldering. Flesh
on fire smells like something disoriented,
a creature running blind.

This is the wake for all things lost.

Like comfort, which has sunk into the mud
along with the body and the lie
that someone else will save you.

Press. Your body's still drumming.
A wound needs pressure to stop
its overflowing.

## Dana
### The Cabin in the Woods (2012)

I never wanted this. Never
tried to be good, or pure.
They asked for sacrifice,
an offering

of the body, never mind
my mind.

To keep this world turning,
unchanging,
on its axis. Never mind
that it's broken.

They asked for slaughter
and all I could say was

*No.*

Drag it all down
into the muck and fire.

See how it rises up.

So maybe this is how
the world ends:
not with a bang or a whimper,
but with revolution.

The promise of something new.

# Sophia
*A Dark Song* (2016)

Are these hyacinth blossoms hanging on
the air? Can I pluck them, stark
as newborn stars, down into this world?
Jewel my hair with dewy petals, dark
as amethyst.

The secret is this: magic isn't magic.
I can lay salt to stave off insanity, cruel spirits,
unwanted gods. But if I lay my hands on you,
will you falter? Dissolve beneath my palms
and leave me gasping bare?

When the signs begin to conjure themselves,
birds shattering into glass and smoky
handprints on the door, when I feel
blood burning at the back of my throat
and grief is a wild dog

snapping jaws alongside my neck,
will I find you there still? If time is a circle
then I've been here before. Do you understand
yet? It's sacrifice, brutal and it leaves you
staggering.

If this is too savage and beautiful to bear,
I'm sorry. The sea holds bodies too
tired to swim, but there's no ending for me
here. I will bathe myself in golden light
like water. I will live.

# Acknowledgments

I'd like to thank the people who had a hand in making this labor of love a reality:

My dear friend Natalya, for reading all of these poems as I was writing them and giving me constant feedback and encouragement.

My dad, for believing in this book even more than I did, and for pestering me until I finished it. Also for making me his business partner and for having a financial stake in this book.

My husband Corey, for always supporting my strange passions, and for talking me off the ledge more than once this year.

My friends, especially my female friends, who do things big and small that give me hope for the future.

The characters who served as inspiration for this book, and the people who invented those characters in the first place.

And all of the women activists, politicians, artists, and writers who are working to create a better world for the next generation of women.

# About the Author

Claire C. Holland is a poet and writer from Philadelphia, currently living in Los Angeles. She received her BA from Washington College in English and creative writing, with a concentration in poetry. She has been a freelance writer for more than ten years.

When she's not writing, Claire can most often be found reading young adult novels or binge-watching horror movies with her husband, Corey, and Wheaten Terrier, Chief Brody. She is also a feminist, a tattoo collector, and an enthusiast of all forms of art strange and subversive.

# One Last Thing...

If you enjoyed this book (or even if you didn't), please consider posting a review on Amazon or Goodreads to help spread the word. Nothing helps an indie author more than reviews and word of mouth, and it is always deeply appreciated. Links to these pages can be found at the author's website:

www.clairecholland.com

Made in the USA
Columbia, SC
12 April 2018